# SPACE • SCIENCE

# Constellations

## Steve Goldsworthy

MEDIA ENHANCED BOOKS
AV2 BY WEIGL
ADDED VALUE • AUDIO VISUAL

www.av2books.com

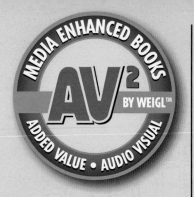

AV² provides enriched content that supplements and complements this boo
Weigl's AV² books strive to create inspired learning and engage young min
in a total learning experience.

## Your AV² Media Enhanced books come alive with...

**Audio**
Listen to sections of
the book read aloud.

**Key Words**
Study vocabulary, and
complete a matching
word activity.

**Video**
Watch informative
video clips.

**Quizzes**
Test your knowledge.

**Embedded Weblinks**
Gain additional information
for research.

**Slide Show**
View images and
captions, and prepare
a presentation.

**Try This!**
Complete activities and
hands-on experiments.

**... and much, much more**

Go to **www.av2books.com**,
and enter this book's
unique code.

## BOOK CODE

J651134

**AV² by Weigl** brings you media
enhanced books that support
active learning.

Published by AV² by Weigl
350 5th Avenue, 59th Floor
New York, NY 10118

Website: www.weigl.com   www.av2books.com
Copyright ©2012 AV² by Weigl

Library of Congress Cataloging-in-Publication Data

Goldsworthy, Steve.
 Constellations / Steve Goldsworthy.
   p. cm. -- (Space science)
 Includes bibliographical references and index.
 ISBN 978-1-61690-633-7 (hardcover : alk. paper) -- ISBN 978-1-61690-637-5 (softcover : alk. paper)
 1.  Constellations--Juvenile literature.  I. Title.
 QB801.7.G655 2011
 523.8--dc22
                            2010050409

Printed in North Mankato, in the United States of America
2 3 4 5 6 7 8 9 0  16 15 14 13 12

042012
WEP160412

Weigl would like to acknowledge Getty Images and NASA as its primary photo suppliers for this title.

**SENIOR EDITOR:** Heather Kissock
**ART DIRECTOR:** Terry Paulhus

# Constellations

## CONTENTS

# Sky
## Pictures

Thousands of years ago, people first noticed that certain bright stars in the sky seem to be grouped together. "Connecting the dots" of these stars, people saw a pattern that looked something like a picture. The picture might be of an animal, a person, or an object. These groups of stars came to be called constellations.

By observing constellations, early scientists noticed that the stars and constellations appeared to move across the sky during the night. They also saw that the sky in summer looked different from the sky in winter.

These changes helped scientists understand some basic facts about Earth. One is that Earth is constantly moving in two different ways. It turns, or rotates, taking 24 hours, or one day, to do this. It also circles the Sun, taking a year to go around once. The first type of motion causes the constellations to move across the sky during the night. The second type is why certain constellations may be visible at some times of year but not at others.

The shimmering lights in the night sky have always been a source of wonder.

The effects of Earth's rotation show up in some photos of the night sky. These photos are made with a camera that collects light for a long period of time in order to make a picture. In such pictures, the light from stars looks like streaks instead of dots.

The stars in the sky on one side of Earth are different from those on the other.

## BRAIN BOOSTER

More than 3,000 years ago, the ancient Babylonians, in what is now Iraq, were the first people known to make catalogs, or lists, of stars. The Babylonians identified groups of stars with specific objects in nature. One of these groups is the constellation now called Scorpius, which looks like a scorpion.

# The Northern and Southern Skies

**W**hile the constellations seem to move across the sky during the night and in the course of the year, they always stay in the same positions relative to one another. Orion, for instance, always can be found between the constellation Taurus, also known as the Bull, and the constellation Canis Major, or the Great Dog. It is as if the entire sky moves, carrying the constellations along with it. A sky chart, or star chart, is a map showing the arrangement of constellations in the sky as seen from a certain place on Earth, such as the North Pole or the South Pole.

Depending on the season of the year and the time of night, many of the constellations visible at the poles can be seen at other locations. Charts of the northern sky show constellations visible in many northern hemisphere countries, including the United States. Charts of the southern sky contain constellations visible in the southern hemisphere.

## GET CONNECTED

You can download star charts at
http://www.midnightkite.com/starcharts.html.

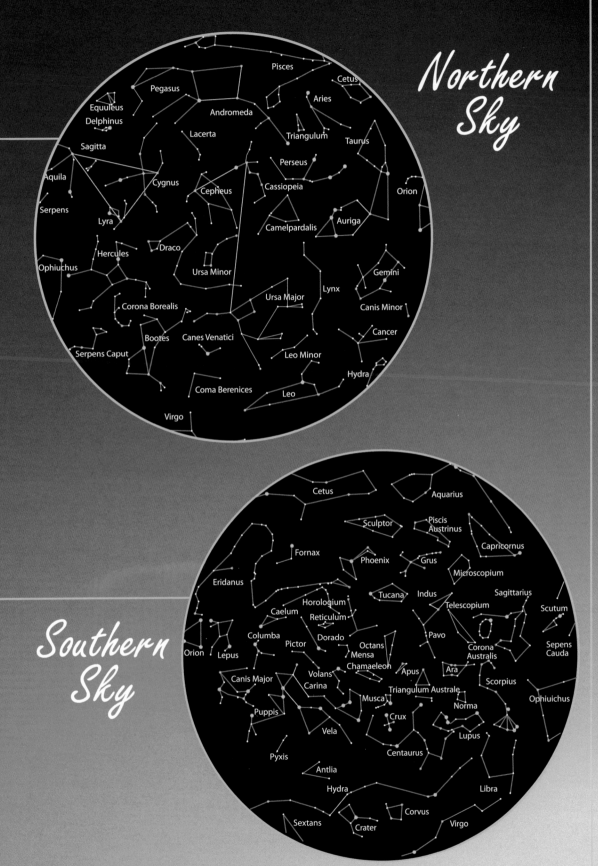

Northern Sky

Southern Sky

# A Star
## Is Born

The stars that make up constellations look like twinkling dots of light. Actually, they are massive objects. Each star is a gigantic glowing ball of **matter** held together by the force of **gravity**.

Scientists think that stars are born in huge clouds of dust, hydrogen, and other gases. If a region of the cloud happens to become denser, or thicker, than other parts, its gravitational force will become stronger. As a result, it will attract more and more matter.

The pale band of light known as the Milky Way may look like a cloud when seen with the unaided eye. It actually consists of billions of stars.

As the mass continues to get denser because of gravity, the temperature within it rises. At some point, it gets hot enough for processes called **thermonuclear** reactions to take place. The mass is now a full-fledged star. The thermonuclear reactions cause the star to give off large amounts of energy. This energy takes the forms of heat, light, and radio waves.

Some stars produce more energy than others. Exactly how much they give off depends on factors such as how much matter they contain and how old they are. Small red stars called red dwarfs are relatively cool. They consume their hydrogen slowly and may shine for tens of billions of years. A large hot blue star consumes its hydrogen at a much faster rate and has a shorter lifetime.

By viewing the sky in infrared light, it is possible to see deep into the dust clouds where stars are born.

**BRAIN BOOSTER**

The heat and light that come from Earth's star, the Sun, make possible the existence of life on Earth.

The temperature inside a hot blue star may be as high as 45,000° Fahrenheit (25,000° Celsius).

# Constellations
## in Ancient Times

**P**eople have been seeing patterns in the sky for thousands of years. The ancient Egyptians were already charting the stars more than 5,000 years ago. By observing the movements of the stars and planets, they created a calendar with 365 days, much like the one used by most of the world today. Based on their observation of the sky, the Egyptians could predict when the Nile River would flood, which was essential for their crops.

A number of today's constellations reflect patterns that the Babylonians identified in the stars. They saw, for example, a lion and a crab. Their lion became today's constellation called Leo, which is Latin for "lion." The Babylonians' crab became today's Cancer, Latin for "crab."

The ancient Greeks developed instruments called astrolabes to determine the positions of stars and planets at different times and places. Astrolabes included a sky map and parts that could be moved to select a location and time of year.

Astrolabes continued to be used for hundreds of years after their invention by the ancient Greeks.

The Greeks also made star catalogs that remained in use for hundreds of years. The names that are used today for the planets, some stars, and some constellations come from the names of Greek gods and **mythical** figures, or from Roman versions of these names. The constellation Orion, for instance, is named after a hunter in Greek mythology.

Hipparchus, who lived in the second century BC, was one of the greatest of the ancient Greek astronomers.

The oldest known sculpture showing constellations identified by the ancient Greeks is from the second century AD. A drawing of the sculpture was made for a book about the stars in the early 1900s.

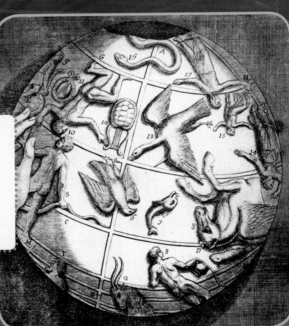

## THINK ABOUT IT
Different cultures do not always see the same patterns of stars in the sky. Look at some famous constellations and see if you can "connect the dots" to form new images. Do you see animals? Buildings? People? Get a star chart and pick a random spot. Can you discover your own constellations?

# Star
# Science

From the eighth century to the fifteenth century, many Arab scientists in the Middle East and North Africa studied the stars and constellations. These scientists made important contributions to astronomy, or the scientific study of objects in space. The Arabs created the first real research **observatories**. These are buildings where scientists carry out astronomical observations.

Galileo improved the telescope and used it to make several important astronomical discoveries.

Modern-day astronomy began around the sixteenth and seventeenth centuries. Galileo Galilei, who lived in Italy, was one of the key scientists in that period. He improved on the telescope, which had recently been invented. Galileo's telescope made it possible to see objects such as stars and planets with surprising detail.

Like other sciences, astronomy is a series of discoveries made by people who built on the work of those who came before. With improvements in observation methods and instruments, astronomers learned that the sky is much more complex than ancient peoples imagined. Some of the objects that the ancients saw turned out not to be individual stars at all. Some were discovered to be the gigantic collections of stars known as **galaxies**.

One of the greatest scientists of all time was Isaac Newton, who lived in England. In 1668, he built the first reflecting telescope. In addition to lenses, the reflecting telescope used curved mirrors to reflect the light coming from the object being viewed. This gave a much clearer image than Galileo's telescope. The reflecting telescope also allowed for the use of much larger lenses. The larger the lens, the more light it can gather. This led to the ability to observe stars at much farther distances. Newton also developed a theory, or explanation, of the way gravity works.

Unlike Newton, modern astronomers tend to specialize in either observation or theory. Observational astronomers look at objects such as stars using telescopes or other instruments. Theoretical astronomers come up with a theory to explain some aspect of an object in space. They base their new theory on scientifically observed facts, calculations, and known theories that are already well accepted.

Isaac Newton introduced the reflecting telescope and stated the principles of how objects move in space.

**THINK ABOUT IT**
Science involves asking questions about the discoveries and theories of previous scientists. What questions would you ask about the sky? Do you want to know about the importance of telescopes? Or do you like imagining what lies beyond the visible stars? Ask yourself, "Would I rather be an observational astronomer or a theoretical astronomer?"

# Mapping
## the Sky

Since ancient times, scientists have made maps of the sky showing constellations and important stars. Modern scientific mapping efforts began with the British astronomer William Herschel in the eighteenth century. He explored the distribution of stars in the sky. Herschel spent several years counting the stars he observed with his telescope. He ended up with a rough idea of the shape of the Milky Way, at least as it looks from Earth.

William Herschel made hundreds of telescopes and surveyed the stars.

Herschel's largest telescope had a mirror 48 inches (122 centimeters) wide. It remained the biggest in the world for half a century.

Later efforts to study the sky came up against a basic problem. Dozens of different systems for mapping the constellations had been developed over the centuries. As the world's scientists increasingly shared scientific information, it became more important that all astronomers use the same description of the sky in order to avoid confusion.

In 1919, astronomers from around the world formed the International Astronomical Union, or IAU, which is based in Paris, France. The IAU developed an official map of the sky. It settled on a list of 88 official constellations. Based on these 88, the IAU divided the **celestial sphere** into 88 regions named after the constellations. This made it possible to give a precise, official name to any star in a region. For example, the bright star known as Polaris is located in the constellation Ursa Minor. Its official name is Alpha Ursae Minoris.

Scientists use a grid pattern to identify locations on the celestial sphere. It works just like the system of latitude and longitude on Earth.

BRAIN BOOSTER

Some of the IAU's 88 official constellations represent objects used by scientists or people in daily life. One example is Antlia, or "Air Pump." Others include Formax, or "Furnace," and Pictor, also known as "Painter's Easel."

Stars are not the only objects in the sky that can receive a name associated with a constellation. For example, there is small, or dwarf, galaxy in the region belonging to the constellation Ursa Minor. It is called the Ursa Minor Dwarf.

# Notable
## Constellations

The International Astronomical Union recognizes 88 official constellations. Here are some of the best known ones.

CANIS MAJOR

GEMINI

| CONSTELLATION NAME | MEANING OR IDENTITY | BRIGHTEST STAR |
|---|---|---|
| Andromeda | Mythological daughter of Cassiopeia and wife of Perseus | Alpheratz |
| Aquarius | Water Bearer | Sadalsuud |
| Aries | Ram | Hamal |
| Cancer | Crab | Al Tarf |
| Canis Major | Great Dog | Sirius |
| Canis Minor | Lesser Dog | Procyon |
| Capricornus | Sea Goat | Deneb Algedi |
| Cassiopeia | Greek mythological queen | Shedir |
| Centaurus | Centaur | Rigel Kentaurus |
| Corona Australis | Southern Crown | Alphekka Meridiana |
| Corona Borealis | Northern Crown | Alphekka |
| Crux | Southern Cross | Acrux |
| Draco | Dragon | Etamin |
| Gemini | Twins | Pollux |

**PEGASUS**

**ORION**

| CONSTELLATION NAME | MEANING OR IDENTITY | BRIGHTEST STAR |
|---|---|---|
| Hercules | Roman mythological hero | Kornephoros |
| Leo | Lion | Regulus |
| Libra | Balance | Zubeneschamali |
| Orion | Greek mythological hunter | Rigel |
| Pegasus | Greek mythological winged horse | Enif |
| Pisces | Fishes | Alpherg |
| Sagittarius | Archer | Kaus Australis |
| Scorpius | Scorpion | Antares |
| Taurus | Bull | Aldebaran |
| Ursa Major | Great Bear | Alioth |
| Ursa Minor | Lesser Bear | Polaris |
| Virgo | Virgin or Maiden | Spica |

**URSA MAJOR**

**URSA MINOR**

# The Zodiac

Throughout history, people observing the heavens have paid particular attention to a strip of the sky known as the zodiac. The zodiac follows a curved line called the **ecliptic**. This is the path that the Sun appears to trace against the background of the stars over the course of a year. A dozen constellations lie on the zodiac. Sky watchers long ago noticed that if they kept track of the Sun's progress from one constellation to the next, they could predict when the seasons would begin each year.

The 12 constellations lying on the zodiac are Aries, Taurus, Gemini, Cancer, Leo, Virgo, Libra, Scorpio, Sagittarius, Capricorn, Aquarius, and Pisces.

The zodiac is important not just as the path of the Sun. The paths traveled by the Moon and the planets in the sky also follow it. Astronomers often make use of the zodiac in describing the locations of these objects in the sky.

## BRAIN BOOSTER

The official IAU constellation called Ophiuchus crosses the ecliptic. It, however, is usually not counted among the traditional constellations of the zodiac.

**Astrologers** divide the zodiac into 12 equal parts called "signs." The signs were originally related to the 12 constellations of the zodiac. Today, the constellations and signs do not always correspond. One reason for this is that the constellations do not occupy equal spaces along the ecliptic.

# Other Star Patterns

One of the best-known star patterns in the sky is known to North Americans as the Big Dipper and to many Europeans as the Plough. It is actually not a constellation. It is an example of an asterism. Asterisms are star groupings that are distinct patterns but are not official constellations. The Big Dipper consists of seven bright stars that belong to the constellation Ursa Major, or Great Bear.

Some asterisms consist of stars from more than one constellation. Stars from the constellations Aquila, Cygnus, and Lyra form the Summer Triangle. The triangle is made up of the brightest star in each of the three constellations.

The Big Dipper provides an easy way to find Polaris, the North Star. The two stars at the end of the dipper's "cup" point to Polaris.

The South Pole is at the point where a line from the Southern Cross constellation meets a line coming straight out from between the two bright "Pointer Stars."

# Constellations
# in Navigation

For thousands of years, people have known that the stars move across the sky in a constant and predictable way. Sailors and travelers long ago learned they could rely on the stars for directions. There were no landmarks on the sea, but bright stars in the sky could help fill this role.

Navigation by the stars, known as "celestial navigation" or "astronavigation," was a necessity for sailors. They could determine their position by measuring a star's altitude, or angle above the horizon. By comparing that figure with the predicted altitudes for specific locations on Earth, they could learn their position. Finding a particular star is easy for people who know the constellations. All they have to do is look for the constellation to which the star belongs.

An instrument called the navigator's sextant was developed in the eighteenth century to measure star angles above the horizon. Much larger instruments called sextants were already being used by astronomers. The navigator's sextant, which made use of mirrors, was small and portable.

For centuries, some scientists used huge astronomical sextants to help find star positions.

One example of celestial navigation involves determining latitude by measuring the angle between Polaris and the horizon. Polaris is always located above the North Pole. For a person at the North Pole, Polaris would have an altitude of 90 degrees. If a sailor in a more southern location measures the angle to Polaris as just 20 degrees, then his or her latitude is 20 degrees north of the equator.

Modern-day navigators use more sophisticated instruments. Many of these instruments rely on the **satellite**-based Global Positioning System, or GPS. GPS devices run on electricity. The sextant, which uses no electricity, remains a valuable backup.

A modern navigational sextant is a compact piece of precision equipment.

# Dark Cloud
# Constellations

Constellations made up of stars are not the only kinds of patterns in the sky. Some cultures have focused on shapes defined not by the light of bright stars but by the lack of light. These shapes are sometimes called dark cloud constellations. Such a shape is formed by massive clouds of dust and gas that block the light coming from stars located behind them. They generally are most visible when they appear against a bright background, such as the Milky Way. The dark areas of the Milky Way are particularly visible in the southern hemisphere of Earth, in places such as South America and Australia.

The Snake Nebula in the constellation Ophiuchus is an animal-shaped cloud that can be seen in the northern hemisphere.

The Quechua people and the ancient Incans of Peru imagined the Milky Way as a river or road. They identified animals in the Milky Way's dark clouds. These animals included a jaguar, snake, fox, and toad.

Some Aboriginal people of Australia see a dark cloud constellation that they call the Emu. It reminds them of a large Australian bird that has that name. The Emu is situated in the region of the Southern Cross and Scorpius constellations. A cloud called the Coalsack **Nebula** makes up the bird's head.

The small dark Horsehead Nebula, in the constellation Orion, can be spotted with a telescope.

The middle of the Milky Way includes areas that are covered by dark clouds.

# Careers with
# the Stars

Scientific study of the stars and other objects in the sky depends on the work of specialists. Some specialists observe and explain **celestial bodies**. Others design and work with the equipment used to carry out the observations. Both types of jobs require a background in math and science. An ability to work well with others is also important. Many jobs involve the cooperative efforts of a group of people. In addition, good communication skills are a necessity. Researchers must be able to describe their ideas and findings clearly. Designers need to explain how to build the equipment they designed.

## ASTRONOMER

Astronomers spend much of their time analyzing the images and data captured by powerful instruments located on Earth or in space. They make use of virtually the entire **electromagnetic spectrum**, including not only visible light but also infrared **radiation**, ultraviolet light, radio waves, x-rays, and gamma rays. Even with the powerful computers available today, astronomers may spend days, weeks, or more processing and studying the data and images delivered by their instruments. Some astronomers work at research institutes. Many others work at colleges or universities and teach as well as conduct research. Astronomers generally have a doctorate degree in astronomy or physics.

## ASTROPHOTOGRAPHER

Astronomy relies heavily on astrophotography, or the photography of stars, planets, and other celestial bodies. Astrophotographers need a knowledge of both astronomy and photography. Some images are made with a camera that detects visible light and is hooked up to a telescope. Others are made with instruments that detect parts of the electromagnetic  spectrum other than visible light. Whatever type of detecting device is used, the image data will likely undergo processing by sophisticated computers. Astrophotographers need to be familiar with the software and hardware involved.

## OPTICAL ENGINEER

Optical engineers design equipment that makes use of light. They play a key part in developing the lenses, mirrors, and other devices used in modern astronomical instruments. In addition to their design work, they may be involved in building and testing the devices. Their field is a highly specialized branch of engineering. Their training typically includes 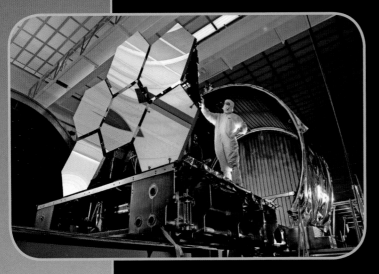 at least a bachelor's or master's degree in engineering or a related area, along with study of the properties of light. After getting a job, they generally continue their education in order to keep up with new developments in optical engineering.

# Not Just for
# Scientists

**S**cientists are not the only people who explore the mysteries and beauties of the stars and constellations. Sky watching can be an exciting hobby. It is open to anyone with an imagination and a sense of wonder. Many amateur astronomers even make contributions to scientific knowledge about the sky. They chart stars, track comets, and discover previously unknown objects.

In the nineteenth century, for example, British amateur astronomer Andrew Ainslie Common helped pioneer astrophotography. He was the first person to show that stars too faint to be visible to the eye through a telescope could be seen in photographs made using a long exposure. In this technique, light is allowed to enter the camera for a considerable length of time to record an image.

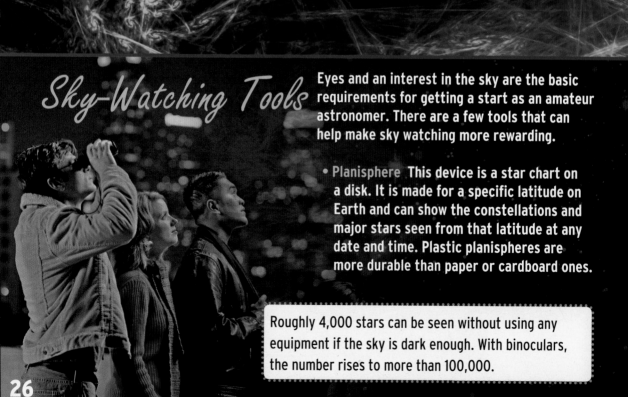

## Sky-Watching Tools

Eyes and an interest in the sky are the basic requirements for getting a start as an amateur astronomer. There are a few tools that can help make sky watching more rewarding.

• Planisphere  This device is a star chart on a disk. It is made for a specific latitude on Earth and can show the constellations and major stars seen from that latitude at any date and time. Plastic planispheres are more durable than paper or cardboard ones.

Roughly 4,000 stars can be seen without using any equipment if the sky is dark enough. With binoculars, the number rises to more than 100,000.

Today, radio telescopes often use an antenna shaped like a dish. The first radio telescope with a dish antenna was built in 1937 by amateur Grote Reber in his Illinois backyard. In 1996, Japan's Yuji Hyakutake, using binoculars, discovered one of the brightest comets of the twentieth century.

Planispheres have been useful aids for night-sky watchers for centuries.

• **Binoculars** A good set of binoculars reveals many more stars and other objects in the sky than can be seen with the unaided eye.

• **Telescope** A portable telescope can reveal more than binoculars. Plenty of small but powerful telescopes are available.

• **Star charts** Up-to-date star charts provide many more useful details about the sky than a planisphere. Sets of star charts in print form are sometimes called star atlases. Computer programs that show the sky in great detail are also available.

## GET CONNECTED

Learn more about amateur astronomy at http://www.backyard-astro.com.

# Test Your Knowledge

**1** What makes constellations seem to move across the sky during the night?

*Earth's rotation*

**2** What does the constellation Leo represent?

*A lion*

**3** The zodiac is usually considered to have how many constellations?

*Twelve*

**4** What is the brightest star in the constellation Canis Major?

*Sirius*

**5** What made reflecting telescopes different from earlier telescopes?

*Use of mirrors*

**6** What kind of star pattern is the Big Dipper?

*An asterism*

**7** What is the official name of the star Polaris?

*Alpha Ursae Minoris*

**8** In what constellation can the Snake Nebula be found?

*Ophiuchus*

**10** What is a planisphere?

*A circular star chart*

**9** What are dark cloud constellations?

*Patterns in the sky formed by dark clouds of gas and dust*

# Glossary

**astrologers:** followers of astrology, or the belief that the positions of stars and planets in the sky can influence people and events on Earth

**celestial bodies:** objects in space such as stars or planets

**celestial sphere:** the imaginary sphere, or ball-like shape, formed around Earth by the sky; to a person looking at the sky, all the visible celestial bodies appear to the eye as if they lie on this sphere

**ecliptic:** the path that the Sun appears to trace against the background of the stars over the course of a year

**electromagnetic spectrum:** the entire range of energy that moves through space in the form of "electromagnetic" waves, such as light, infrared radiation, radio waves, and x-rays

**galaxies:** huge groupings of stars that are held together by gravity and may number in the millions or billions

**gravity:** a pull that objects or any bits of matter exert on one another

**matter:** any material or substance

**mythical:** referring to traditional stories, often from a religious or sacred point of view, that are meant to teach a lesson or reveal a truth

**nebula:** a giant cloud of dust and gas in space

**observatories:** buildings or sets of telescopes and other instruments that astronomers use to carry out observations

**radiation:** a process in which energy travels from an object through space, such as sunlight

**satellite:** an object in orbit around a planet or other body

**thermonuclear:** referring to processes involving the joining together of the nuclei, or cores, of the particles of matter known as atoms

# Index

# Log on to www.av2books.com

AV² by Weigl brings you media enhanced books that support active learning. Go to www.av2books.com, and enter the special code found on page 2 of this book. You will gain access to enriched and enhanced content that supplements and complements this book. Content includes video, audio, web links, quizzes, a slide show, and activities.

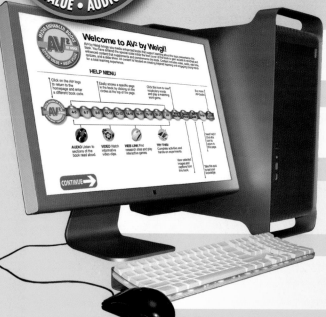

## Audio
Listen to sections of the book read aloud.

## Video
Watch informative video clips.

## Embedded Weblinks
Gain additional information for research.

## Try This!
Complete activities and hands-on experiments.

# WHAT'S ONLINE?

|  Try This! |  Embedded Weblinks |  Video | EXTRA FEATURES |
|---|---|---|---|
| Complete engaging activities that further explain constellations. | Learn more about constellations. | Watch a video about constellations. |  **Audio** Listen to sections of the book read aloud. |
| Write a biography about an important person. | Find out more about a notable person. | Check out another video about constellations. |  **Key Words** Study vocabulary, and complete a matching word activity. |
| Test your knowledge of space. | Learn more about pursuing a career studying constellations. | | |
| Play a fun interactive activity. | Find out more about the technology used to study constellations. | |  **Slide Show** View images and caption and prepare a presentati |
| | | |  **Quizzes** Test your knowledge. |

AV² was built to bridge the gap between print and digital. We encourage you to tell us what you like and what you want to see in the future.

## Sign up to be an AV² Ambassador at www.av2books.com/ambassador.